DK ESSENTIAL MANAGERS

Doing Business in India

DEAN NELSON

London, New York, Melbourne,
Munich, and Delhi

Senior Editor Peter Jones
Senior Art Editor Helen Spencer
Executive Managing Editor Adèle Hayward
Managing Art Editor Kat Mead
Art Director Peter Luff
Publisher Stephanie Jackson
Production Editor Ben Marcus
Production Controller Hema Gohil
US Editor Chuck Wills

Produced for Dorling Kindersley Limited by

cobaltid

The Stables, Wood Farm, Deopham Road,
Attleborough, Norfolk NR17 1AJ
www.cobaltid.co.uk

Editors Louise Abbott, Kati Dye, Maddy King,
Marek Walisiewicz
Designers Darren Bland, Claire Dale, Paul Reid,
Annika Skoog, Lloyd Tilbury, Shane Whiting

First American Edition, 2008

Published in the United States by DK Publishing
375 Hudson Street, New York, New York 10014

08 09 10 11   10 9 8 7 6 5 4 3 2 1

DD474—November 2008

Published in Great Britain by
Dorling Kindersley Limited.

A catalog record for this book is available from
the Library of Congress.

ISBN 978-0-7566-3708-8

DK books are available at special discounts
when purchased in bulk for sales promotions,
premiums, fund-raising, or educational use.
For details, contact: DK Publishing Special Markets,
375 Hudson Street, New York, New York 10014 or
SpecialSales@dk.com.

Color reproduction
by Colourscan, Singapore
Printed in China by WKT

Discover more at **www.dk.com**

Contents

CHAPTER 2

Understanding business etiquette

CHAPTER 3

Getting things done

Introduction

In 1991 the Indian government announced a U-turn in economic policy. The country examined and learned from the strategies of the Southeast Asian "tigers"—Singapore, Malaysia, Indonesia, and Thailand—and vowed to do better. India is now the world's second-fastest growing economy and its second most populous, with incomes and exports leaping forward year on year.

This is a market that is willing to do business with the rest of the world—but in its own way. While India is deceptively Western in some respects—such as its use of international English as a main language—it retains a uniquely Eastern character. Whether you are looking to start up your own business, find an outsourcing partner, or create a joint venture, an understanding of the country's history and culture is essential for achieving business success.

This concise book provides you with an overview of the country and all the practical information you will need to make decisions, avoid costly pitfalls, and get started. Find out how to recognize and deal with the implications of the caste culture, how to manage the older and younger generations—who have vastly different priorities and expectations—and where the best opportunities for business lie. From negotiating and managing to setting up or partnering a business, this book has all you need to get started in this exciting market.

Chapter 1

Business profile

Why has India become so important in global business? There are two overriding reasons: it is enjoying massive market growth with almost unlimited potential; and it is home to the world's largest pool of skilled and professional workers. Understanding the business environment that India presents requires some knowledge of the country's history and politics.

Arriving in a land of contrasts

The business traveler's initial reaction on arriving in India is often one of bewilderment: can this really be the world's second-fastest growing economy? Confusion is understandable in a country that seems at once familiar, exotic, and unnerving.

Technological transition

India is an assault on anyone's senses. A traveler setting foot for the first time in New Delhi, Mumbai, or Kolkata will be struck by the chaos and apparent poverty. But beyond the chaos is a country that is catching up fast, and in many areas racing ahead. Its basic infrastructure—roads, electricity and water supply, and public transportation—appears to be trapped in the 19th century, while its information technology and communications often leave the West trailing in its wake: in India can you receive emails in remote villages that are accessible only by mule train.

THINK DIVERSE
Remember that there is no such thing as a single "Indian culture." The country is incredibly diverse, with some areas adopting Western values while others retain a tribal organization.

India has placed enormous value, backed by practical resources, into knowledge and technology. Its heavy investment in training—the country produces more than three million university graduates a year—has transformed India into one of the world's leading growth centers for software development, IT outsourcing, biotechnology, and research and development. Its skilled workforce has also led it to become the outsourcing hub of the world, particularly for customer services and design.

Analyzing the market

India is many countries, with many languages and cultures, which were all thrown together by British colonial rule and later transformed into one national identity after Independence in 1947. Since then, and especially since 1991, when India began relaxing state control of industry and opening the country to foreign investors, its consumer market has grown exponentially. While the story of the last 20 years has been about India's integration into global supply chains, its new story is about huge domestic consumption and intra-regional Asian trade—particularly with China. This is a market that businesses cannot afford to ignore.

 IN FOCUS... MULTIPLE LANGUAGES

First impressions may be misleading. You will notice the widespread use of English, which is the language of politics and commercial operations. However, the official national language is Hindi (spoken by 30 percent of nationals), and there are 18 regional languages. One compromise has emerged with the blending of English and Hindi into "Hinglish," which is the real language of India's middle class. However, India's films and TV shows have made Hindi the dominant language of the region, and it is increasingly displacing languages in other South Asian countries as they are flooded by Indian media and news of its film and sports stars.

Country profile

India is—after China—the second most populous country in the world, and its largest democracy. A nuclear power with its own space program, India retains a huge, largely illiterate rural population.

Capital/largest city: **New Delhi/Mumbai**

Population: **1.12 billion**

Official languages: **Hindi and English are official national languages; there are also 18 regional languages**

GDP/GDP per capita: **US$1,000 billion (2007)/US$965 (based on exchange rate) or US$2,700 PPP***

Currency: **I rupee (INR) = 100 paise**

Time zone: **UTC +5.30 hours**

Dialing code: **+91**

Principal business areas: **New Delhi, Mumbai, Kolkata, Chennai, Bangalore**

***PPP**—*Purchasing Power Parity is a measure of the purchasing power of a currency relative to the US dollar.*

The great divide

India is home to both the world's richest and poorest people. By 2008, India had 53 US$ billionaires—and more billionaires in the world's top 10 than any other country. However, it is also home to more than a quarter of the world's poor. While the middle class is becoming wealthier, 900 million people still live on US$2 a day, with 400 million survive on one dollar a day. The Indian government is aiming to make growth more inclusive, and to this end is focusing spending on education and health.

Choosing India

The reasons for doing business in India are compelling: India has experienced extraordinary growth since 1985, doubling the average household disposable income and creating a new and huge middle class with considerable purchasing power. It has a low-cost, competitive workforce and its government is actively pursuing a progressive reform process, with investment-friendly policies and a visible commitment to education and training.

Predicting the market

By 2025, India's population is expected to rise to around 1.4 billion; economists predict that average income will triple over this period. India's huge middle class, currently standing at around 50 million, will increase to around 600 million, triggering explosive growth and making India the fifth-largest consumer market in the world. The middle class will dominate spending, controlling around 59 percent of India's consumer market. While income growth has been—and will continue to be—fastest in urban areas, rural incomes are also set to grow. These traditionally poor rural households are likely to enjoy the same standard of living and rate of consumption as today's urban households by the year 2018.

CULTURAL ANTENNAE

Dealing with poverty

At some point in your trip, you will come face to face with the country's poor. You may have your sleeve tugged by an amputee, or be asked for charity or "baksheesh" by a woman holding a sleeping baby. They are a harrowing fact of Indian city life and giving or not giving is regarded as a personal decision—Indians will not criticize your decision either way. But focusing on this issue with potential business partners in India may often be interpreted as running down the country and questioning their sense of justice and compassion. Save the poverty debate for your friends back home.

Backing a winner

TARGET YOUR MARKET

Around 60 percent of India's highest earners live in the eight largest cities—and this is not expected to change over the next 20 years. These top-end customers are a highly visible and easily targeted market segment.

India has become the second most desirable target for overseas investors. Foreign Direct Investment (FDI) is allowed in all but the most sensitive of areas, such as defense, and totaled US$15.7 billion in 2007. Significantly, FDI will continue to play a key role in economic growth—the share of FDI in total investment more than doubled from 2.55 percent in 2003–2004 to 6.42 percent in 2006–2007.

Shifting demographics during economic growth will bring unique challenges to businesses. They will need to attract and retain new consumers in large numbers, and establish brand loyalty despite the changing tastes of increasingly wealthy customers. Managing this shifting market will require flexibility and vision, but the potential rewards are enormous.

TARGETING YOUR INVESTMENT

The 10 sectors that attracted the highest FDI into India during 2007–2008

- Construction
- Telecommunications
- Drugs and pharmaceuticals
- Transportation industry
- Fuels (power and oil refineries)
- Electrical equipment (including computer software)
- Construction
- Chemicals (other than fertilizers)
- Services sector (financial and non-financial)
- Food processing industries
- Housing and real estate

History and business

The people of the Indian subcontinent have been trading with Arabia and Greece for several millennia. Commerce flourished under Mughal rule, and by the 16th century India controlled more trade than the whole of Europe. In the 18th century India and China were the world's largest manufacturing economies, but by the time it gained its independence from the British Empire in 1947, India's share of world income had been reduced to just 3.8 percent.

TIP

BE PREPARED FOR QUESTIONS

Indians possess and express a natural curiosity and love conversation. Don't be surprised if a total stranger introduces himself and engages you in discussion. Be polite and keep an open mind.

The socialist legacy

After Independence, India followed the socialist policies of its first prime minister, Jawaharlal Nehru. The main industries were state controlled, foreign investment was limited, and trading in shares heavily restricted. The results were mixed. India developed powerful domestic industries and home-grown brands, protected from Western competitors, but their products were poor-quality and the country's infrastructure suffered from low investment. In 1991 the Indian government took steps to liberalize its economy and to begin dismantling the so-called "License Raj"— the state control that gave civil servants and politicians the power to decide which companies would run which industries. The reforms amounted to an economic revolution.

Rapid reforms

The prime minister of 1991, Narasimha Rao, relaxed state controls, opened up key sectors to foreign investment, and allowed international companies to hold controlling stakes in key joint ventures and 100-per-cent ownership in certain sectors. He introduced a privatization program, relaunched the country's capital markets, and allowed Indian companies to raise funds overseas. The impact of Rao's reforms was extraordinary: in just four years investment rose by US$5 billion.

Domestic brands

Since liberalization, Western brands from Pepsi to Nike have flooded into India, and Indians have shown an insatiable appetite for them. But despite the allure of Western products, India has developed its own, new domestic brands that have become widely trusted. Tata and Mahindra SUVs dominate roads that were once hogged by the Hindustan Ambassador—the stately Indian-made car of the 1950s—and Indian brands such as Infosys and Hero Honda are beginning to appear on the international stage.

CULTURAL ANTENNAE

The last rupee
Decades of hardship have had a lasting impact on India, infusing its attitude to trade and money. Millions of Hindus and Sikhs from western Punjab fled to New Delhi after Independence, arriving penniless. Slowly they rebuilt their business empires in New Delhi, watching every rupee, fearful that the new wealth they had created could again be taken from them overnight. It is not uncommon, even today, for wealthy Delhiites to repair their own clothes and homes to save a few rupees—and for the younger generation of wealthy middle-class Indians to joke about their parents' and grandparents' thrift.

Planning your activities in India

India is a subcontinent similar in size to the European Union. It stretches from the tropical rainforests of Kerala and Tamil Nadu in the south to the high Himalayan peaks in the north. It is a land of wildly varying and sometimes extreme weather, the effects of which are magnified by poor infrastructure and power supply. Working within the dictates of climate and location is not just sensible—but essential.

TIME YOUR TRIP SUCCESSFULLY

Where possible, plan your trip during the coolest, driest months. This is when it is easiest to travel, and it is also the wedding season, when you may be invited as an honored guest—an invaluable opportunity for relationship building.

Watching the weather

Climate should be a serious consideration when you plan your business trips to India; during the summer heat and humid monsoon months, India suffers the most power cuts, and doing business away from five-star hotels may become difficult.

Avoid visiting the northern plains—including the cities of New Delhi, Lucknow, Chandigarh, and Amritsar—from April to June, when they experience temperatures of 115 °F (46°C) or higher. Even the ever patient Indians can lose their temper in the extreme heat, and it is not conducive to fostering successful business relationships. If you need to meet with Indian partners during the summer, it is worth remembering that India's middle-class business families often flee to the cooler climes of the old British hill stations, such as Mussoorie in the north, or Ooty in the south. Inviting them to visit your home country may be especially welcome at this time.

Toward the end of June the monsoon brings relief from the heat, but its spectacular rains flood the roads and bring transportation to a standstill. The most benign weather runs from September to April, when temperatures and humidity levels plunge to those of a European or American spring or summer.

Key business areas

A. NEW DELHI
Investment opportunities: software, IT-enabled services, high-tech industries, small-scale industry.
Timing your visit: summer temperatures can be brutally hot; winters are cold, and flights are often affected by fog. Visit from mid-October to mid-December and mid-January to April.

B. MUMBAI
Investment opportunities: automobiles and components, biotechnology, floriculture, food processing, textiles, leather.
Timing your visit: avoid the monsoon season from mid-June to September when floods bring the city to a halt. Visit from November to February, when humidity levels fall and days are pleasantly warm.

C. BANGALORE
Investment opportunities: India's IT hub; computer software, telecoms, automobiles, food processing, floriculture, biotechnology, tourism, infrastructure projects.
Timing your visit: one of India's best climates. Avoid October, as thunderstorms cause flooding and power cuts. Visit from December to February.

D. CHENNAI
Investment opportunities: engineering, automobiles, software, IT-enabled services, biotechnology, healthcare, pharmaceuticals, tourism, textiles.
Timing your visit: avoid May and early June, when temperatures skyrocket, and the city suffers from power cuts and water shortages.

E. KOLKATA
Investment opportunities: agriculture, tourism, IT, metals, petrochemicals, food processing.
Timing your visit: avoid May, the hottest month punctuated by violent storms and June to September, when monsoon rains flood the crumbling former capital almost daily.

Business, caste, and culture

India's Hindu majority is sharply divided into "castes" or classes, which in theory prescribe the social and career prospects open to a person. The caste system is one of the most divisive social and political issues facing India today: understanding its structure and relevance to society will ease many of your business interactions.

TIP

CHECK NAMES BEFOREHAND

Check someone's surname carefully before meeting them: names can reveal background and religion. The suffix "-jee" (as in Banerjee) is a sign of high caste; Patel, Iyer, Mudaliar are all caste names. The surname or middle name of "Singh" denotes a member of the Sikh faith. Note that the rigid hierarchy of caste is less relevant to the new, younger employees of today.

Knowing the boundaries

There are four main castes—Brahmins (priests and teachers), Kshatriya (kings, warriors, and aristocracy), Vaisya (traders), and Sudra (laborers, servants). Dalits, or "untouchables," are considered too "unclean" to even be a formal part of the system. Caste can be an indicator of wealth or power, but it is unreliable. The author of India's constitution, Dr. B. R. Ambedkar, was an "untouchable"; there are Dalit millionaires and chief ministers; there are political alliances between Dalits and Brahmins; and some Brahmins now live in poverty.

Working with the caste system

Caste issues may sometimes explain rigidly hierarchical attitudes and conflicts among staff—especially where team members are required to work very closely together. While ideas of caste should not be indulged, you need to be aware of creating potential conflict; if you appoint a Dalit as a team leader, any Brahmins on the team may have difficulty accepting their orders.

As a manager, you need to stress that career advancement is based on performance—not status or longevity—and that employee rights are applicable to all castes and genders. Ultimately, however, Hinduism is a practical religion, and caste will rarely stand in the way of a good deal.

Religious community

India is one of the world's most ethically diverse countries; around 80 percent of the population is Hindu, but there are also many Muslims, Sikhs, Jains, Buddhists, and Christians—all with different approaches to business. Hinduism is a highly practical faith that sets great store by the acquisition of wealth. It is common to see shopkeepers and other business people begin each day's work with a prayer to Ganesha, the elephant-headed god who removes obstacles, or Lakshmi, the goddess of wealth and luck. Almost all new business ventures in Hindu India begin with prayers for Ganesha's blessing, and it is common to offer a Ganesha statuette as a gift to anyone setting out on a new project.

India's Muslim minority has a thriving business community, but a different approach to wealth and more restrictions on the manner in which money is made. Islam does not allow involvement in money-lending, and forbids the charging of interest. Consequently, Muslims in India have largely left banking and financial services to the Hindus. But religious obligations have not stopped Indian Muslims becoming some of the world's richest and most successful entrepreneurs. Azim Premji, CEO of Bangalore-based Wipro, one of India's biggest software companies, is an Ismaili Muslim who has amassed a fortune of US$17 billion.

The knowledge economy

India's higher education system is so successful that one of the government's biggest fears is a "brain drain" of top university graduates to high-paying jobs overseas. While the government is considered not to have delivered in primary and secondary education, its higher education establishments—in particular the Indian Institutes of Management and Indian Institutes of Technology—are the envy of the continent.

Recruiting the elite

FIND THE SMARTEST GRADUATES

India's brightest young management prospects start looking for jobs in January and February, when the country's top companies launch recruitment drives.

India has more graduates—around 40 million—than most countries have people. Many are drawn from the elite fee-paying schools of the main cities and the old-style boarding schools, most of which are first class. It is increasingly common for "non-resident Indians" (NRIs) living in the West to send their children home to India for a high-quality, inexpensive, boarding-school education. Those who win a place at an Indian university are, by definition, the elite. A place at New Delhi University, especially St. Stephen's College, known as "India's Oxford," or Jawarharlal Nehru University—regarded as one of the best in the world—is often seen as preferable to one at a university in the US or Europe.

IN FOCUS... LEADING LIGHTS

India's seven Institutes of Technology, or IITs, specialize in engineering and science. They were founded in the early 1950s to speed up the country's technological development. Today they are ranked third-best in the world for technology after MIT and Berkeley. Despite their success, there has been criticism that many graduates went on to seek work in other countries. However, with India's spectacular growth and development, this situation is now reversing, with many highly qualified graduates returning to India, or remaining in the country after graduation.

But it is India's management and technology institutes that have won the plaudits, and attracted global recruitment companies. Seven Indian Institutes of Technology (IITs) were created by the government during the late 20th century, and there are plans to open a further eight. Admission to the institutes of management and the institutes of technology is highly competitive; this, coupled with rigorous academic practice and natural proficiency in English, produces the highest-caliber graduates. Recruiting these people is not cheap; in 2007–2008 it was common for high-fliers to be paid first salaries above US$100,000 and five-figure "signing on" bonuses.

CASE STUDY

The power list

The Indian Institutes of Technology have produced some of the world's most influential leaders in information technology and science. They include:

- Nandan Nilekani and Narayana Murthy, founders of Infosys, now one of the world's biggest IT companies
- Vinod Khosla, founder of Sun Microsystems
- Lord Kumar Bhattacharyya, Professor of Manufacturing Systems at Warwick University, UK, and advisor to the British Prime Minister
- Krishna Bharat, principal scientist, Google
- Ramanathan V Guha, inventor of RSS, which allows blogs, news feeds, and podcasts to be regularly updated
- Arjun Malhotra, founder of HCL Technologies, one of India's top IT service companies and a major player in the BPO call center sector.

Finding the opportunities

People at every level of Indian society are enjoying an increase in wealth and purchasing patterns are changing fast. This translates into an ever-evolving set of business opportunities—in meeting domestic demand, manufacturing for export, or engaging with government. Opportunities are currently greatest within the areas outlined below.

Business Process Outsourcing (BPO)

India's best-known success story has been the rise of its call center or BPO sector. If you are looking to outsource company services, India offers considerable cost benefits together with a highly educated, English-speaking labor force. Increasingly it can also offer a faster speed to market. The BPO sector is developing rapidly: although initial contracts were based around low-end, non-core activities, such as customer support services, BPOs are moving up the value chain. Consider outsourcing to India if you are looking to outsource knowledge processing research, finance, insurance, accounting, marketing or legal services, or infrastructure technology—network or systems management and asset management. The newest areas include software development and computer animation.

Steel

The speed and scope of India's development has led to soaring demand for steel, leading the country's industry to expand even faster than in the rest of the world, where it is growing rapidly. India is an underdeveloped steel market with great potential: the Indian Ministry of Steel envisages a demand of 90 million tons by 2020. There are opportunities for companies to build steelworks, as POSCO is doing in Orissa, or to contribute to their construction. If your company is involved in engineering, there are opportunities within the mechanical, metallurgical, industrial, electrical, and civil fields. The government is also eager to source foreign investment: it allows 100 percent FDI for metallurgy and processing under the simpler, quicker automatic route.

Communications

Telecom is another of India's big success stories, and there is still room to be a part of it. Every year 10 million new subscribers in India are tempted by cheap call charges and new payment services, and the market is set to grow—the mobile phone remains most people's primary point of connectivity, rather than PCs.

If your business lies in phone sales, bear in mind that although the market is huge, it is uniquely demanding: Reliance proved successful by selling cheap, affordable handsets to India's lower middle classes and poorer workers. There are still considerable opportunities for content providers, as these services are in high demand, especially those focusing on Bollywood music.

Infrastructure

The Indian growth story has highlighted its poor infrastructure. Billions of dollars are now being poured into new airports, ports, roads, pipelines, rail improvements, power stations, and water-treatment plants, and this work is open to foreign firms. Opportunities are best for larger companies that have the experience, skills, and technology to manage big projects, such as the greenfield development of airports. There are prime opportunities for engineering and construction firms in almost every part of the country. If you are looking to buy or start a construction business in India you will also benefit from the government's desire to increase foreign participation: it allows 100 percent foreign-equity participation in the construction industry.

Power

Electricity is arguably India's most exciting investment prospect. The country plans to bridge a 15 percent shortfall in supply by 2012 by building "ultra-mega power plants" around the country, and by buying up oil and gas concessions around the world to fuel them. India does not allow private utilities to generate nuclear power, but there are opportunities for firms to supply equipment: General Electric and Areva were bidding for contracts worth several US$ billion in 2008. The government is eager to promote investment in power plants, coal plants, natural gas processing plants, and renovation and modernization of existing thermal and hydro power plants. Many opportunities exist for engineering or consulting within the transmission and distribution sectors.

SEIZE THE DAY

India's real estate sector is in an early growth stage—an ideal time to join the market. The industry is now worth around US$16 billion a year and FDI in the sector rose from 4.5 percent in 2003 to 25 percent in 2006.

IT and software

India's IT industry is world class. By the start of the 21st century it had grown into a global leader worth more than US$50 billion, expanding at triple the national growth rate. Multinationals have been quick to see the opportunities, investing over US$10 billion in 2006–2007: growth of over 20 percent a year continues to make this sector very attractive. If you want to set up an IT business in India, consider siting it in a SEZ or Software Technology Park to take advantage of tax exemptions for foreign companies, well-qualified employees, and well-above-average infrastructure. If you're looking for a partner to develop software, an Indian company is worth considering— IT companies have proven that they are able to innovate and invent as well as trade.

Real estate

India's property markets are increasing in value. Demand is growing, fueled by the presence of non-Indian firms, the globalization of larger Indian corporations, and the increasing wealth of the domestic market. Demand for property outstrips supply across all segments, and there are wide opportunities whether your business lies in residential, commercial, retail, or hospitality assets. Changing markets are leading to new opportunities: commercial spaces are shifting from sale to lease-and-maintain models, mortgage financing is penetrating widely across urban areas, the luxury housing segment is expanding at around 25 percent a year, and the entry of international players is heating up the retail market.

Pharmaceuticals

The Indian pharmaceutical industry is the fourth largest in the world, and one of the fastest growing. By 2010 its domestic market is expected to be worth US$10 billion, with exports at around US$18 billion. International players, such as Pfizer and Glaxo SmithKline, and bio-agriculture companies Monsanto and Aventis, have already opened offices in India to take advantage of the many domestic and export opportunities. If your business operates in this sector, an Indian arm of the company would allow you to benefit from the availability of low-cost, high-quality production; low research costs; access to research scientists at around a quarter of the costs of those in the West; and world-class testing facilities.

Opening global gateways

Indian companies are fast becoming innovators, investing in research and development, but they are also globalizing—making foreign acquisitions to open new markets and buying research and design capacity. At the same time, European, American, and Asian corporations are becoming ever more interested in buying a stake in India's firms and future—which may be an important gateway to all the emerging countries in the east.

Plugging in to the East

In 2006–2008, mergers and acquisitions between Indian organizations and international firms were a constant news story. In 2007 alone, the Indian corporate sector was involved in deals worth US$60 billion. The trend was led by Tata's takeover of the Anglo–Dutch company Corus, and Vodafone's buy-out of Hutch, India's leading mobile phone operator. Cisco, which opened up its Eastern headquarters in Bangalore in 2007, was motivated to do so because of India's talent pool and its domestic market, but also because of its global position—both geographical and political. At the opening of the firm's new offices, CEO John Chambers acknowledged India's unique position as an entry point to Asian markets, saying: "We came to India for growth in all the emerging countries and the talent that's here. We're focused on this engine for growth. This country understands how to partner."

CASE STUDY

India's autos on the world stage

For years, talk of India's car industry summoned up images of the stately Hindustan Ambassador sedan, which remains the vehicle of choice for government ministers. But in Spring 2008, two events forced the world to think differently about India's auto future. The first occurred when Ratan Tata, the visionary head of one of India's most powerful corporates, unveiled the "Nano," finally realizing his dream to produce a "one lakh (US$2,500) car." This sleek, 624cc, four-door micro car was hailed as a triumph of design and fuel economy. Its low price has caused excitement in India, where it is cheaper than an auto-rickshaw, and also overseas, where it has caught the wave of interest in cost-conscious green motoring. Tata is not the only Indian company making first-class cars—Mahindra's Scorpio SUV is world class, and Maruti is a market leader—but it is the first to beat Western rivals in research and development, and the first to demonstrate truly global ambition. The second event occurred only weeks later, when Tata announced that it had bought Land Rover and Jaguar—two of the world's most iconic car brands—from car giant Ford.

Joining resources

Organizations from some countries have taken the decision to insure against the prospect of a world dominated by a hi-tech India, by creating "partnership" agreements to develop new innovations and products with partners in India. For example, in 2008, academics from Indian and British universities joined forces with leading engineering and IT firms to develop new wireless networks and laptops, with the aim of bringing affordable technology to India's rural poor. Projects include a US$50 laptop that runs on negligible electricity: this has the potential to transform the use of technology by organizations as diverse as village councils and national stock exchanges. Similar agreements have been made between the Indian government and overseas administrations to cooperate in certain areas of science and technology, such as developing applications for research in nanotechnology and nanomedicine.

TIP

LEARN TO COUNT IN LAKHS

When you begin doing business in India, you will have to learn to count all over again. India has its own numbering system for large sums. A lakh is one hundred thousand rupees, and is written with two commas: 1,00,000. A crore is ten million, written: 1,00,00,000. A billion is called an arawb. Most investments are reported in crores.

Chapter 2

Understanding business etiquette

Your first meeting with your partner is a cultural minefield, but as a foreigner, you'll be accommodated and allowances will be made. An understanding of Indian etiquette, however, will show you are serious about forging a longer-term relationship.

Establishing hierarchies

When Indians meet business contacts they try to establish exactly where their companions stand in the hierarchy of power and status. This "sizing-up" process is not unique to Indians, but it is performed with an unashamed ruthlessness that may be unfamiliar to you.

TIP

PLAY THE NAME GAME

Refer to your business partner by title or surname unless they specifically invite you to use first names.

Meeting and greeting

Your partner's religious background will determine your opening gambit: for a Muslim, say "Salaam Aleikum" and offer a handshake; but for Hindus and others, use the ritual greeting of "Namaste" (hold your hands together upward at chest height as if in prayer, while saying "Namaste"), followed by a handshake. If your business partner is a woman, this greeting is friendly without overstepping any boundaries. Don't read too much into a weak handshake; it is the most common in India. Don't be offended either if your Indian partner offers you a wrist to shake instead of a hand—some people will do this as a mark of respect if for some reason they don't feel their hands are clean enough or worthy to shake yours.

After your initial greeting, offer your business card with your right hand—the left is considered unclean—and receive your Indian partner's with courtesy. Read it and then put it carefully in a wallet to show that it is important to you. Address your partner by the correct title; if it is Professor, Doctor, or Colonel (retired), he or she will be very proud of it.

No business can be done before the power relation is established and an etiquette of appropriate deference is established: who is the superior, and who the subordinate? This is generally decided through a series of questions that can be direct and even brutal—especially for a newcomer to India—but it is an essential ritual that betrays the country's obsession with status and hierarchy.

TIP

PROJECT YOUR STATUS

Your business card is an important part of a first impression. Use it to signal your status, and include not just your company position but any senior academic title. On the reverse side, give your details in Hindi—although your partner is certain to be fluent in English, it will be taken as a sign of respect.

BUILDING YOUR CREDIBILITY

FAST TRACK

OFF TRACK

FAST TRACK	OFF TRACK
Bringing a colleague to the meeting to take notes and assist you	Being shy, modest, or humble
Stressing your academic title and qualifications (more so if female)	Turning up to a meeting without knowing exactly who will be there
Establishing who the decision-maker is among your Indian partners, and focusing on them	Ignoring hierarchical culture: forgetting to greet senior and older people first
Being calm, patient, and respectful—letting your partner decide when to cut to the chase	Leaving the meeting without saying goodbye to each member of the Indian team individually

Cementing business relationships

In India, business is about building relationships and long-term trust. But these relationships are not quite the same as those in Western business—Indians do not distinguish between social friendships and business relationships. Developing a "friendship" is a necessary part of making a deal and forging a business relationship.

KNOW YOUR PARTNER'S GOAL

While your goal during negotiations may be a signed contract (gained as fast as possible, because time is money), your Indian partner may primarily be seeking to create a relationship between the two companies. The contract expresses that relationship, but the "deal" is the relationship itself—and this takes longer to achieve than a simple financial agreement.

Establishing friendships

When you meet your Indian business partners, be prepared for grand hospitality, and accept it on the understanding that you will be expected to return the kindness. You may be told: "you are like a brother/sister to me"—this is a form of flattery called *Chamchagiri*, which binds business partners closer together. You too can play the game—call your partner *Bhai-saheb*, which means "respected older brother." The journey toward this level of intimacy may be slow but it cements an essential level of trust.

Playing safe with conversation

Indians care deeply about how the world regards them and their country. As a business visitor you should show that you respect and admire India: contain some of your first impressions and avoid questions about social problems, which will make your Indian partner feel embarrassed. Focus instead on the growing number of positives. Ask about India's impressive Space Program, its pioneering role in IT innovation, its global takeovers, or its cricket team.

Building trust the Indian way

- Avoid contentious issues, such as caste, class, and gender

- Tell your Indian partner about your family life at home

- Ask about your partner's family

- Show an interest in Indian culture

- Be patient with older family members in your partner's company

- Express your desire to achieve a long-term win–win alliance with your business partner

- Hold back: let your partner decide when to cut to the chase in a deal

- Don't show irritation if your partner is late or takes other calls during talks

- Keep your temper in check, even if you are provoked

- Don't hurry your partners into talking terms of business

Recognizing corruption

Corruption is so widespread in India that the country is often described as "institutionally corrupt." But it would be wrong to see the role of bribery as solely a monetary issue. India is a highly deferential society, and corruption is also a symbol of one's place in the hierarchy: the size of bribes offered to an official are yardsticks of his or her power.

TIP

PREVENT CORRUPTION IN YOUR VENTURE
Practice transparency and record-keeping in all your business activities. Move transactions online where possible to reduce the human element necessary for corruption.

Corruption and authority

In a 2005 survey by the anti-corruption campaign group Transparency International (TI), more than 60 percent of Indian respondents said they had paid bribes to government officials. The police department was judged to be the most corrupt, followed by the judiciary, land administration, especially building plan approvals, and municipal services, such as electricity.

As a foreigner, you may never actually see or know about bribes demanded for permissions related to your business projects in India—it may be handled entirely by your Indian partner. However, if you are directly sounded out about a bribe payment, you have a tough decision to make. It is a fact of life in India that speeding your paperwork through the bureaucratic jungle often requires cash incentives for those who carry it through to the permission stage.

CULTURAL ANTENNAE

The etiquette of corruption
The manner in which a bribe is solicited often emerges naturally in the context of a brush with officialdom. If you meet a civil servant whose permission you need for some part of your venture, he may ask where you are from, and when you reply, he may say: "I love that city. I haven't been there in years." This is usually a cue for you to say: "You must come soon, in fact, I will arrange it. Just let me know when you're planning to go." If you do not rise to the bait, the meeting may end abruptly, the official may lose interest in your case, and your file may languish at the bottom of a tall pile.

Corruption in practice

Offering a bribe, or receiving one, is illegal in India, and may also be a domestic offense in your home country. However, it remains a very real dilemma for many foreign business travelers, especially when time is short and officials are obstructive. It is not uncommon for this dilemma to be "fudged" by the appointment of an agent who charges you a fee to process applications on your behalf and takes care of various "commissions." The good news is that while corruption in India is widespread, there is evidence that it is declining. Privatization of utilities and an increase in online applications for government services have played a part, and the introduction of the Right to Information Act has made officials more accountable than ever before.

IN FOCUS... REASONS FOR CORRUPTION

Recognizing why corruption occurs in India can help you prevent the practice in your business, and help you spot new opportunities:

- Outdated infrastructure: employees operating with inadequate support may be unable to offer services to all who apply; corrupt practices introduce a hierarchy of service.
- No incentives: low-paid staff experiencing heavy workloads have no incentives, other than bribes, to increase their work rate.
- Political interference: service providers become demoralized by interference from politicians and resort to taking bribes.
- No staff training: employees feel unable to cope with the increased demands and expectations of consumers that have occurred in many business sectors.

Managing negotiations

In India, haggling is a way of life, and everything works backward from the price you are willing to pay or accept; almost all strategies that serve that outcome are considered acceptable. There are some general principles and protocols that must be followed, but politeness and immense patience are the most critical qualities for successful negotiation.

TIP

READ THE SIGNALS

Indians dislike saying "no," and you may have to interpret their body language and analyze their comments in order to establish what they are really saying. Look for hints—if the Indian team suggests that there remain many issues to solve, or that they will "try" to do something, they are probably saying "no."

Negotiating at a slower pace

Indians expect negotiations to be personal, friendly, and positive. Language is more flowery, flattery is expected by both sides, and personal chemistry is a necessary catalyst in striking any deal. Here are some pointers about what to expect in your negotiations:

• Multitasking is part of the culture; your meeting may be interrupted by phone calls or people walking in with questions. Do not allow this to affect you.

• Be prepared for your negotiations to take much longer than would be normal in your own country.

• The Indian team will subject your proposal to microscopic scrutiny, pointing out every weakness and flaw in the greatest detail. Do not show anger or impatience throughout this process: wait until you have an opportunity, then re-state your proposal with detailed justifications for each of your terms. Throughout this your Indian hosts will listen politely, and then, probably, reject all of your points.

• Keep the mood light and non-confrontational, but do not concede your position.

The closing stages of a negotiation often come unexpectedly just as you are beginning to lose hope of any conclusion. The moment of agreement is easy to miss because there may have been many handshakes, but not a definitive one. Look out for a marked relaxation in behavior from your hosts, and a sudden sense of ease in the atmosphere.

Reaching an understanding

Indian companies will often expect negotiations to begin after you have accepted their tender to supply a service—only then will you discover that the tender was offered as an application to be a preferred bidder. Contracts themselves are not considered legally binding. Even if signed under a Western country's jurisdiction, your Indian partners will regard a contract more as a flexible statement of general intent. Be prepared for this and try to leave some margin for flexibility—it is a good investment in sustaining a longer-term relationship.

BRING A COLLEAGUE

Take a colleague with you to any meeting where you need to take notes. If you're seen to take notes yourself, the Indian decision-maker will assume that you're only an emissary for a greater authority at home, and won't treat you as an equal.

MEETING FOR RESULTS

FAST TRACK

OFF TRACK

FAST TRACK	OFF TRACK
Asking your Indian partners where to sit at a meeting—they'll want to seat you opposite the lead decision-maker	Sitting down anywhere, before you have understood the hierarchy of the Indian team
Beginning with social discussion, and allowing the Indian team to bring the conversation around to business	Talking about the business in hand immediately
Drilling down from the broad picture of who your company is and your general aims to specific aims, and reasons for this meeting	Once you're talking business, focusing immediately on the problem in hand, asking how quickly and at what cost the work can be done
Following your Indian partners, should they stand up, when senior members of their team enter the meeting	Remaining seated if the Indian team stand up as a new (senior) member enters the meeting
Directing all your questions and comments to the lead decision-maker	Directing your comments to people in support roles

Assessing your partner

If you are considering a joint venture, acquisition, merger, or Foreign Direct Investment (FDI) proposal, you need to be sure that your partner is honest and reliable, and that you have correctly assessed any potential liabilities. This is most important in India, where corruption is rife.

Performing checks

*Due diligence—
*the investigation,
by investors, into
the details of a
deal and partner;
the verification of
material facts.*

If your business partner is of any size, check their credentials in internet, newspaper, and magazine articles as well as business databases and public records. If your partner is a relatively new or small company, they may not yet have a paper trail; in either case, you should conduct a formal due diligence* exercise. This may raise suspicion and discomfort for smaller firms with no international experience, but explain to them if necessary that companies from other countries have different disclosure obligations and regulatory requirements.

TIP

CHECK PROPERTY STATUS
You can check the ownership and legal history of any Indian property in the Registrar of Properties. Contact the Registrar of Companies (ROC) to check whether a property is free of mortgages or other loans.

Being thorough

If you are asking your potential partner to complete a voluntary self-disclosure document, it is important that the answers are self-warranted as true and attached to your contract or joint venture agreement with indemnities if they are later found to be false. However, you may choose instead to appoint a company to carry out a due diligence process for you. In either case this process should include an investigation into the company's business interests and commercial track record, and any political affiliations, litigation history, or criminal history, or any pending liquidation or recovery proceedings against the company or its directors.

What due diligence addresses

- Severance plans
- Pensions
- Company accounts
- Labor union involvement
- Share capital

- Licenses and permits
- Share options
- Exports and imports
- Taxation issues: customs/excise, sales tax

- Intellectual property rights
- Environmental issues
- History of legal proceedings
- Shareholders

- Directors' interests and affiliations
- Contractual liabilities
- Company assets
- Company business interests

TIP

GO SEE FOR YOURSELF

Always insist on visiting company plants—you will learn more from on-site conditions and practices than you could ever learn from information on paper.

Using data rooms

Larger companies in India now use data rooms for conducting due diligence, especially when competitive bidding is taking place between several interested parties. Until recently, this involved placing all relevant data in a physical room, and allowing all interested parties equal access at an agreed time and date. However, technological developments and the increasing number of cross-border mergers and acquisitions have led to the development of virtual data rooms, where the information can be accessed online. These have many advantages if you wish to buy into an Indian company: they can be accessed from your home country, saving time and travel; they provide fast "search" facilities; data is available 24/7; and non-disclosure disputes are minimized. However, if you use this system for due diligence on a company, bear in mind that you may be granted different levels of access from other buyers, and also that the vendors are able to track your activity on the site. This may provide them with more information about your level and areas of interest than you would like.

Using government protection

According to the World Bank, investor protection is better in India than for the region in general, and on a par with OECD (Organization for Economic Co-operation and Development) countries. Transparency of transactions in India is greater than that of the 30 member countries of the OECD.

If you are forming a joint venture, consult with the National Foundation for Corporate Governance for the latest regulations and guidance on Indian best practice. Ask your partner to sign up to a "nothing to hide" statement of intent that will bode well for your future relationship.

Understanding politics

As a foreign business visitor, you may never come into contact with India's politicians, but you do need to be aware of their pervasive role in Indian society, and that they can be of help or hindrance to business. Politicians regularly get involved in matters beyond their remit: intervening with local power officials, for example, when they threaten to disconnect electricity cables to slums where power theft is rife. The officials invariably concede.

Contact with politicians is as much a dilemma as with corrupt officials. Having a relationship with a senior politician will raise your status considerably, and may make business easier—there will be fewer problems if you are known to have powerful connections. But you must also consider the wisdom of becoming less remote and more engaged in local matters, and whether it is another matter best left to your Indian partner.

 IN FOCUS... THE BIG BROTHER STATE

Although the post-1991 economic reforms have scaled back the so-called "License Raj"—where politicians decided who controlled many industries—the decisions of politicians continue to shape the landscape of Indian business. Billions of dollars of trade will be impacted by the government's decision on whether to allow foreign supermarkets to open in India, for example. Vast sums are also at stake in the government's decisions on low-tax Special Economic Zones—how many will be approved, the scale of the developments, and who will win tenders to build them.

The Hindu Undivided Family business

More than 70 percent of India's market capitalization is in the hands of family businesses. While this is not entirely unusual, the Hindu Undivided Family business (HUF) is unique, and operates under very particular rules and restrictions. It is crucial to understand how these companies operate if you are to do business with them.

Keeping it in the family

Most Indians live in "Hindu joint families," where several generations of the male line live under one roof. The eldest male is usually the head of the family and of the family business. Many of the biggest Indian businesses are family dynasties run along the HUF model, though there are signs of change, notably in the IT sector. HUFs can be secretive and inward-looking, with senior positions chosen for family reasons rather than merit. Work continues 24/7; policies are discussed at the dinner table; middle-management is often weak or nonexistent; and little career progression is on offer. If you are seeking a distribution contract, an HUF with a good reputation may be ideal, but for joint ventures you need to ensure that your partner is open to Western ideas of transparency, merit, training, and promoting talent.

CULTURAL ANTENNAE

Thinking as a family

A recent survey found that 46 percent of Indian businessmen felt their successor should be a relative, compared with 22 percent in North America. Just under 60 percent believed shares should only be held by family members, and over half felt family should receive preferential pay. Very few family members had ever worked outside the family firm before joining it: collectively, they showed a lack of distinction between family, management, and ownership.

Working with the "Kartha"

The HUF is recognized in Indian Hindu law. All male members of the family, known as "co-parceners," operate the business together under the leadership of the head of the family, known as the Kartha. Legally, the Kartha can commit an HUF company to a joint venture, as its representative, but the company cannot commit to anything without him. In effect, any deal is simply done with the Kartha—and he accepts legal responsibility in person when he makes the deal. There is no legal requirement for this kind of business to be registered, although the family still enjoys the same legal rights as non-family firms. While the Kartha alone has the legal right to manage the business, and has unquestioned authority in relation to all company decisions, the family as a whole has unlimited liability for any decisions that are made.

DEALING WITH HUFs

FAST TRACK	OFF TRACK
Appointing independent directors and a remuneration committee	Allowing your partner free reign to run the business in India
Agreeing a human resources and staffing policy focused on merit	Ceding control of appointments to your Indian partners
Strengthening management by appointing a CEO from outside your partner's ranks	Letting your partner's deference culture pervade your joint venture
Encouraging a questioning culture with regular management meetings where decisions can be discussed	Allowing decisions to be made over dinner tables and at family gatherings

Bridging the generations

It is common to hear Indians say "old is gold" in reference to the wisdom that age and experience bring to human enterprise. At the same time you will notice an obsession with the movers and shakers in the 18–28 age group who are filling some of the most lucrative jobs and introducing new management models into India. Take the time to recognize and understand the differences in attitude between these groups—the so-called Guru generation and GenNext—when working with them.

The Guru generation

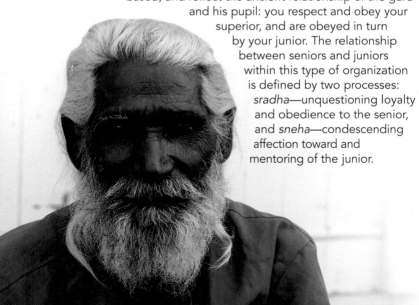

For India's Hindu majority, the older generation, raised either in family businesses or in the pre-1991 government-controlled sector, operates on traditional Hindu organizational values. These are deference-based, and reflect the ancient relationship of the guru and his pupil: you respect and obey your superior, and are obeyed in turn by your junior. The relationship between seniors and juniors within this type of organization is defined by two processes: *sradha*—unquestioning loyalty and obedience to the senior, and *sneha*—condescending affection toward and mentoring of the junior.

GenNext

Globalization and the growth of Indian companies into multinational corporations has driven traditional Indian families to adapt—often by sending their children to the world's best management schools. The young guns of GenNext are likely to have studied at an Indian Institute of Management or Technology, in the US, or in the UK. The result is a young workforce equipped with well-tested Indian negotiating techniques combined with the best of Western management and HR knowledge.

The guru culture and GenNext often coexist within Indian family businesses that have gone global, but in the relatively new IT, BPO, and R&D (Research and Development) sectors the new breed holds sway. They are highly trained, can operate at a cross-cultural level, and make valuable employees, but you will need to pursue a very proactive HR approach in order to find and retain them.

HOW TO...
ATTRACT THE BEST OF THE NEW

Offer European/American-style remuneration and benefits packages

↓

Encourage talent through fast-track promotion schemes

↓

Support creative, sporting, and social activities among staff to promote team affinity

↓

Reward innovation and talent over age and experience

↓

Introduce reverse mentoring, where junior staff can share their ideas and experience with seniors

Understanding India's consumers

India's growing market is huge and complex: it has over 20 languages, and many social strands that are constantly shifting due to income growth, increased exposure to global media, and sea changes in values and beliefs. Companies that understand the complexity of this vast consumer base will be the most successful in the domestic market and can expect to benefit from great economies of scale.

An intelligent market

By 2025, vast numbers of Indians will have risen from poverty to form a middle class of around 600 million people. Domestic consumption is already a major driver of that growth, and there is growing demand for cars, motorbikes, telecommunications, domestic and foreign holidays, healthcare, education, branded clothes, and luxury goods. It is not, however, a virgin market, and foreign arrivals have lost ground by making false assumptions. India's consumers are canny, quality-focused, and price-sensitive, as Motorola discovered when they found no takers for their mobile phones at Rs30,000 ($700). When they cut the price to Rs10,000 ($230), they sold out.

CASE STUDY

Adapting global products

Don't assume that your marketing will translate from one country to another. Kellogg's thought Indians would naturally buy their cold breakfast cereals, failing to appreciate that the Indians love hot parathas, uttapams, and dosas, and strongly dislike the idea of cold food or drink for breakfast. As a result the organization had to build the brand from scratch, and create a market for their products. It now promotes the *shakti* ("power") health and educational benefits of its cereals to Indian parents who want nothing more than for their children to be top of the class.

CULTURAL ANTENNAE

Branded goods

Before 1991, the country's domestic brands had enjoyed more than 40 years of protection and in some cases, a monopoly. This has translated into a preference for Indian brands, even among the younger generation. One survey found that most younger people believed that Indian products were better suited to Indian life, while another found that four of the top five favorite brands were Indian. However, some international brands have overcome this barrier: Honda very successfully partnered with the bicycle manufacturer Hero, and Samsung dominates the white goods market. And when it comes to luxury goods, imported brands fare much better: India, along with Greece and Hong Kong, is one of the top three brand-conscious countries in the world. Gucci and Calvin Klein are massively popular, and the market for co-branded laptops and mobile phones is on the rise.

Urban and rural markets

India's urban population is wealthier than the rural: the average urban income is US$2,250, while people in the country earn less than half of this. But don't ignore the rural market: incomes there are growing at the same speed as those in the cities, and the population is vast—three times as many people live in villages as in the cities. While the urban market accounts for most luxury branded sales, branded basics—such as household cleaning products, refrigerators, stoves, gas, lighting, and televisions— are all selling in increasing volume outside the towns and cities. The rural market is interested in well-priced, practical goods that improve their standard of living. And although the population is scattered over a vast area, wireless internet and mobile communications are well developed and are making the market easier and cheaper to target.

With more than 750 million people and a market in Fast Moving Consumer Goods already overtaking that in the cities, India's rural areas present an unprecedented opportunity for those prepared to invest in researching, understanding, and targeting the market.

CASE STUDY

Why should boys have all the fun?

India is a man's world, but the role of women is slowly changing. In cities, the trend is shifting away from the traditional "stay-at-home" wife to a more fulfilled, working woman who can contribute to the household income. A large number of young women have found work in the BPO sector. More than 60 percent of affluent women are university graduates and post-graduates, while India's highest and lowest social classes report high percentages of women working outside the home. Women are fast becoming powerful consumers in India, and have positive attitudes toward well-known brands and say they would not mind paying extra for them. The Hero Honda Pleasure scooter perfectly highlighted this new desire for independence, offering women a brightly colored, high-comfort scooter with the slogan, "why should boys have all the fun?" The company created all-female showrooms and mechanic teams—and captured 9 percent of the valuable scooter market.

The underprivileged majority

India's rising middle class is not the only driver of growth in the country—some of the biggest market successes have been scored by companies selling to the poor. This market is not one indistinguishable mass, but a differentiated market with considerable spending power: useful, good-value products have created markets where no-one thought they existed. Sahara, a media and financial services corporation based in Lucknow, created a multibillion-dollar empire from para-banking—taking as little as one rupee per week from poor villagers into savings accounts. Today it employs just under a million workers. The Ambani family created a US$45 billion company by buying US$10 mobile phones from China and selling them cheaply to rickshaw pullers and domestic servants throughout India. The mobile phone giant Nokia scored a hit in India by selling a low-cost, dust-proof handset with non-slip strips and a built-in flashlight—it became a firm favorite with India's legion of truck drivers, who found it practical.

Young and old

India is a young country, with a huge population bulge—it has half a billion people under 25 and more than 250 million between the ages of 15 and 25. But almost two-thirds of teenagers are poor and live in the country. The same is true of the 20–24 age group. The relative "big spenders"—of which there are around 7 million—watch MTV, visit multiplex cinemas, hang out in malls, and buy the latest branded games and music players, designer jeans, and grooming products. India's working singles spend an average of $2,671 per year, which goes on essentials, such as food (33 percent), transportation (8 percent), and rent (14 percent). When they marry, their spend dips to $2,509, but more goes on household groceries (38 percent). Money is earmarked for education, books, stationery, music, and communication.

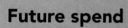

Future spend

India's furious pace of development, rising incomes, increasing urbanization, and huge investment in infrastructure mean private consumption is expected to increase four-fold by 2025 to just over US$1,500 billion. Some anticipated growth areas are:

- Sports club memberships
- Cosmetic surgery
- Education and communication
- Clothing
- Food and drink
- Grooming and beauty products
- Healthcare and household products

Chapter 3

Getting things done

Your success in India will depend on mastering the intricacies of working within government regulations, Indian business law, tax obligations, and the country's infrastructure. This chapter will guide you through the complexities of setting up a business in India, looking at how best to minimize risk and maximize potential profits.

Navigating the regulations

With the right information, you can set up your own enterprise or a joint venture in India very quickly. Knowledge of local and state laws and the right documentation can help streamline the process, while taking advantage of incentivized locations can help you avoid unnecessary costs.

KNOW THE LAW
Hire a reputable Indian law firm to guide you through your obligations. Failure to comply with government regulations can lead to legal action, delays, or even requests for bribes.

Maintaining standards

Don't be tempted to lower your standards when doing business in India. Since 1986, customers in India have been protected by a demanding Consumer Protection Act. All goods must be fit for purpose, delivered on time, and exactly as promised. Deficiencies in service, technical malfunctions, delay or cancellation of delivery, or failure to provide a service that has been paid for are all breaches of this act—and consumers can take their case to a Consumer Forum or a Consumer Court at any time up to two years after the goods or services have been delivered.

Protecting the environment

The Indian government has begun to take its responsibilities toward the environment very seriously; indeed India is the first country in the world to have environmental protection measures enshrined in its constitution. Policies such as "prevention of pollution at source" are enforced by the Central Pollution Control Board, which ensures the "polluter pays" for its own cleanup.

If you are thinking of building production facilities or offices for your company in India, you will need to gain an approved Environmental Impact Assessment (EIA) before any work can begin. Take careful advice—guidelines for and exemptions to EIAs change often. Failure to comply can be extremely costly: several huge mining ventures have been delayed for years because they did not obtain the right consents. Refineries, petrochemical plants, and cement, paper, and dyeing factories need Ministry of Environment approval, and must maintain certain standards on emissions and discharges, and air, water, and soil quality. Directors of companies responsible for actions that damage the environment can be prosecuted.

TIP

GET ADVICE

Contact your government trade department; most countries now have an "Indian Business Council" that can introduce you to potential partners in India. Also contact the Federation of Indian Chambers of Commerce and Industry.

IN FOCUS... UNDERSTANDING TAXES

When choosing whether to operate as a "foreign" or "domestic" company within India, bear in mind that these incur different tax liabilities:

- Companies managed from India are classed as "domestic" and are taxed at around 30 percent of global turnover.
- Companies not incorporated under Indian law are classed as "foreign," and these are taxed at around 40 percent of Indian earnings.

A corporation is resident in India if it is incorporated there or if it is controlled entirely from India. Businesses collect and pay tax using a state sales tax ID number—you can obtain this from the tax department of the state in which your company operates. Your business will also be liable for indirect taxes: the Central Sales Tax (for goods sold inter-state or internationally), and VAT, which varies from 1 to 20 percent.

Dealing with India's infrastructure

The signs of India's rapid growth are all around, but so too is the evidence of how poor infrastructure is constraining it. Power cuts, water shortages, airport delays, overloaded ports, and overcrowded roads are a way of life. India's inadequate infrastructure presents one of the biggest hurdles you will need to overcome in building a successful business.

Working against the odds

India's infrastructure gap is an indicator of its future potential: the government is spending more than US$400 billion on upgrading roads, ports, airports, and power and water supply, to give India four world-class airports, a network of US-style freeways, and the power it needs to drive the economy. Generous tax holidays are available for core infrastructure projects. But the current situation is difficult for business: demand drastically outstrips supply, so electricity is expensive and supply is unreliable.

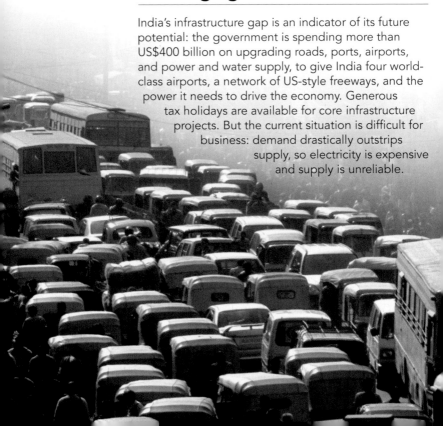

Getting around

Poor transportation links continue to hamper business. Economic losses from congestion were estimated to be as high as US$6 billion in 2007. Large trucks are banned from entering some cities by day, which can add crippling delays. Ports suffer from lack of dock space and cranes, and airports from lack of warehousing. Weather conditions can worsen problems: power fails more often, traffic becomes even more congested, and goods stranded outside—due to lack of warehousing—can be ruined by rainstorms.

CHECK YOUR CITY CHOICE
Each city has varying degrees of problems in different areas of infrastructure—always research the extent of problems in each city that you have short-listed as a potential site.

Coping strategies

Almost every airport, road, and power provider is "sorry for the inconvenience" as they undergo a major overhaul, refurbishment, or rebuild. Your task is to rise above them so you and your staff can focus on the business:

• **Pick your premises carefully:** complete power back-up for a fully air-conditioned office is essential.

• **Choose private sector** telecom providers such as Airtel, Reliance, or Tata Indicom for stress-free communications.

• **Hire English-speaking drivers** (or those of your native tongue) for your fleet, even if more expensive, to make sure you arrive relaxed and in good time for meetings.

• **Engage a resourceful** travel consultant for the best advice on reliable airlines and the safest routes in your areas.

• **Travel business class** on internal flights: the additional cost is minimal in India, and the executive lounges are a sanctuary from the chaos beyond.

Using Indian services

India's services are close to breaking point, and while the laws of supply and demand suggest that the country's infrastructure gap will be filled, any organization doing business in India must—at present—make the best of the situation. Recent legislation has addressed the "leakage" (a euphemism for corruption) that surrounded large infrastructure contracts, and these projects are attracting the attention of Indian and overseas companies that can see the huge opportunities.

MAIL
India's postal service is unreliable and items are often "lost." Use "Speedpost"—considered trustworthy and cheaper than Federal Express—or local or international couriers for important mail.

AIRPORTS
Flying is the fastest way of getting around, despite the age and inefficiency of India's airports. Passenger numbers are growing fast, and the larger cities will all benefit from upgrades soon: Bengaluru International Airport was unveiled in May 2008 and Delhi and Mumbai's new international airports are expected to be completed by 2010 and 2011 respectively.

PORTS
India has 12 major seaports, and over 150 minor ones. There are long delays, and sometimes a lack of warehousing. Investigate your chosen port's facilities in detail, and always build a contingency into your schedules when shipping goods.

WATER

Water, sewerage, and waste disposal are major problems for businesses, especially manufacturers. Water is often rationed and pumped into buildings at fixed times. Some businesses resort to buying water and having it delivered to their premises in tankers.

RAIL

Express and mail trains connect all of India's main centers: look out for the faster, smarter "Shatabdis"—passenger trains that run between large cities. Customer service is improving: you can book online or by mobile phone, and stations are being upgraded. However, rail travel is still an exotic experience.

Navigating transport and utilities

TELECOM

Mobile communications, broadband internet, and wireless and data services in India are world class—true success stories. India is the second-largest wireless market—ahead even of the US.

ROADS

Avoid traveling by road whenever possible. India has the second-largest road network in the world but its record for building and managing multi-lane roads is poor: it is rarely possible to drive for any distance at speeds greater than 25 mph (40 kph) and short distances across urban areas can take many hours.

Managing your money

India's banking sector now meets international standards on asset classification, income recognition, and transparency and disclosure. Its retail sector is extensive and efficient, with online and phone banking making business possible throughout the country.

Knowing the system

India is widely regarded as one of the leading capital markets in the developing world, and it is internationally respected because of its transparency with respect to price information. The country also has well-developed and well-regulated equity, derivatives, exchange, debt, and commodity futures markets. This demonstrates the country's appetite for investment and its market maturity and provides the financial infrastructure necessary for growing and ultimately floating a business.

Setting up finances

Wherever your business is based, you will be well served by banks in India. The country has an extensive network of banks with branches and ATMs serving even some of the country's most remote rural areas. Although the sector remains dominated by the State Bank of India and the Punjab National Bank, the private sector has made great strides in recent years. Most foreign investors choose to work through their own home bank if it has an operation in India. This can make it easier to set up your Indian operation, and borrowing can be secured in India as part of a global limit—for example a global borrowing limit of US$1 billion may have US$100 million earmarked for draw-down in India.

Transferring money

Your bank will make all the necessary arrangements for transferring money. There are limits on personal transfers, but none on transferring money from India for acquisitions overseas. For other transfers, the Reserve Bank of India (RBI)* must be informed of the purpose, and the money must be transferred through authorized dealers—usually your bank. Borrowing money from international markets for your Indian business is subject to a limit of around US$50 million, but the RBI can grant approval for larger amounts.

Using electronic banking

Almost all of India's top banks, including the State Bank of India, offer internet banking to allow you to check balances, make payments, and transfer funds between accounts. Some offer wireless banking from your mobile phone. The bank will issue secure personal identification numbers that allow you to make transfers and pay bills via SMS message.

ASK YOURSELF... WHAT KIND OF BANK DO I NEED?

- Do you intend to run businesses both within India and elsewhere? If so, choose an international bank with a strong presence in India, your home country, and any other target countries.
- How actively do you want to involve your bank in the business? Meet the relationship managers from a short-list of possible banks, and choose the team you feel most understands your business needs.
- How important is access? Does your preferred bank have a network of branches in the areas of India that are important for your business?
- How much support do you need? Will your bank take care of any business documentation required by the Reserve Bank of India? Check on international transfer times, paperwork undertaken, and charges.

Choosing an entry strategy

As a foreign investor wanting to establish an Indian operation, you have several options, from branch offices through to wholly owned businesses. Each has advantages and disadvantages; identify your main purpose and projected length of business before focusing on one type of strategy.

TAKE THE SHORT CUT

Consider hiring an Indian-based management consultant to research your market, or contact your country's embassy in Delhi. Many governments offer advice and arrange business introductions.

Scoping the options

If you want to get a clearer picture of Indian market conditions before committing, establish a "liaison office." This cannot conduct direct business, but can promote the parent company's goods and services, and promote collaboration with companies in India. Liaison offices must have prior approval from the Reserve Bank of India (RBI). Approval is typically granted for three years before renewal is required. If you wish to execute a specific project, the best option is to set up a "project office," which does not need RBI approval, but must close as soon as the project is completed. A longer-term option is to open a "branch office", from which you may conduct import and export business, offer consultancy, render IT and software services, operate airlines and shipping services, and manufacture in Special Economic Zones (SEZs).

IN FOCUS... GAINING GOVERNMENT APPROVAL FOR YOUR BUSINESS

The RBI grants approval for most sectors under the "automatic route," though some sectors still need governmental approval through the Department of Economic Affairs. As a first step, make inquiries at one of the Indian embassies or High Commissions in your country. The caps on investment stakes in different sectors and other investment rules are changing rapidly. Avoid making costly mistakes by hiring an Indian lawyer who specializes in FDI, or make your application direct to the Foreign Investment Promotion Board (FIPB)—even if you believe your planned investment comes under the 100 percent automatic approval category. The FIPB will still advise you and give you a clear ruling.

Subsidiaries

One of the best ways to escape the restrictions placed on branch and liaison offices is to establish a subsidiary, in the form of a private company established under domestic Indian law. The subsidiary is freer to conduct business in India, and can repatriate profits without approval, but there are restrictions on foreign exchange transactions and income tax.

Joint ventures

Joint ventures offer the best opportunity for benefiting from local knowledge and talent, through your Indian partner's local market share, experience, contacts, and distribution network. If the venture is approved by the RBI, and investment enters India through official transfers, capital and dividends can be repatriated overseas without further approval.

Choosing a location for your business

India's rapid growth has given birth to business-friendly areas. First came the business and IT parks, offering modern offices, good connectivity, reliable infrastructure, and leisure centers; and then Special Economic Zones (SEZs), which offer all this plus substantial economic benefits. Weigh up your options carefully before making a decision.

Knowing the benefits

Business parks, IT parks, and SEZs were conceived to take pressure off city centers, whose infrastructures were crumbling under the pressure of India's phenomenal economic growth. The IT and business parks are efficient commercial sites that hold tens to hundreds of businesses. They provide a "work-live-play" environment that includes restaurants, gardens, and gyms, 24-hour security and fire protection, solid infrastructure, streamlined telecom networks, and, in some cases, guaranteed electricity—Bangalore IT Park, for instance, has a dedicated power plant.

Siting your business in one of these parks can also help to solve the most common HR problem in India: retaining valuable staff. The working environment has become a key consideration for employees who are deciding whether to leave or stay with a company. Business park offices are becoming an essential part of the package for highly qualified staff.

IN FOCUS...
FINANCIAL INCENTIVES

Firms operating within SEZs enjoy the following tax incentives:
- Duty-free import or domestic purchase of goods for development or operation
- Exemption from Central Sales Tax
- Exemption from Service Tax
- Exemption from VAT/State Sales Tax
- Variable exemption from Income Tax for 15 years: 100 percent for the first five years; 50 percent for the second five years; up to 50 percent for the third five years.

Making the most of SEZs

SEZs were introduced in 2000 to boost exports. These zones enjoy the same high quality of working and living spaces as business parks, but they are deemed "foreign territory" by the government to enable them to function almost autonomously. Businesses based within SEZs operate under fewer regulations and have to deal with less bureaucracy than those elsewhere—compliance procedures are simplified and rely largely on self-certification. SEZs also benefit from substantial tax concessions—many of the tariffs and quotas are simply eliminated.

TIP

GET A FLYING START
If you are setting up a new business in India, you'll do it faster within an SEZ. You will gain single-window clearance—you won't have to seek clearance from many separate departments, such as town planning, fire service, labor departments, and so on—and you will benefit from faster government approval.

Rolling out the idea

In 2008 there were 600 SEZs in various stages of approval; around half are rooted in the IT industry and most are in the southern and western regions of India, with far fewer in the north and east. Some Indian companies—such as Infosys and Wipro—have bought land to develop entire SEZs for their businesses alone. This option is not open to you as a foreign business, but you can lease space from developers before, during, or after a SEZ build. SEZ units may be used for manufacture of goods or provision of services.

CASE STUDY

Firms at home in SEZs
Reliance Industries has invested US$100 billion in building two new "mini-cities" on the outskirts of Mumbai and New Delhi. The company is building new homes, public transport systems, schools, hospitals, leisure centers, shopping complexes, and factories in its SEZs. The Sahara Group is also planning to build 217 new "townships" throughout India. International companies that have made their homes in SEZs include Nokia, Motorola, and Dell. Nokia, the Finnish telecom company, chose a site in Tamil Nadu where it could base its factory and offices alongside eight of its suppliers for maximum efficiency.

Importing and exporting

For all its growth in recent years, India has a growing balance of payments deficit, and government policy is focused on increasing exports. There are now a number of schemes open to international companies that ease the process and carry considerable cost benefits.

TIP

KNOW YOUR TRADE

Exporting is complex. It is essential that your staff understand the terms of trade as well as the rules and ethics of international trade.

Exporting more easily

Agricultural export zones, export incentive schemes, and duty-free Special Economic Zones (SEZs) are all worth investigating if you are exporting from India. The SEZs provide an environment that is already officially "foreign territory," enjoying exemption from customs and excise duties, as well as reductions in taxes and more liberal rules on domestic regulations and investment.

If you wish to export from India, you will need to register with the Director General of Foreign Trade and obtain an import–export code number. It is also advisable to register with India's statutory Export Promotion Council and Commodity Boards. All exports must be inspected for quality prior to shipment, unless the goods being exported bear the Indian Standards Institute mark, although if you are exporting large quantities of goods, you can apply for a license to self-certify their quality.

The logistics of exporting are complicated by the fact that India's ports and air-cargo warehouses are chaotic and corruption is rife. A freight-forwarding business may be able to save you time and money. These one-stop-shop services deal directly with sea, air, and overland carriers, and offer tracking and communications regarding the shipment. They undertake customs clearance, export and import tax payments, shipping fee payments, trade documentation, and insurance.

Importing goods from India

Whether you import Indian goods through a broker, have a long-term contract manufacture relationship, or employ Indian workers in a subsidiary company, you will need to understand and constantly monitor your supplier's value chain in order to maintain quality and, if appropriate, brand authenticity. Suppliers may sometimes substitute ineffective or even dangerous ingredients or components, attempt to pass off counterfeit-branded merchandise as authentic, or falsely certify that they have met government-mandated safety and labeling requirements. Once your firm's name goes on the package, however, it is you that becomes responsible for any errors or omissions, both legally and in terms of public opinion.

Imports and exports

INDIA'S PRINCIPAL IMPORTS
- Crude oil and petroleum products
- Precious stones and gold
- Capital goods (especially second-hand)
- Chemicals
- Coal

INDIA'S MAIN EXPORTS
- Agricultural products
- Gemstones and jewelry
- Petroleum and engineering products
- Textiles and garments
- Pharmaceuticals
- IT services
- Chemicals

Tapping into Business Process Outsourcing (BPO)

HSBC, American Express, Qantas, and Tesco are just a few of the big names to have taken advantage of India's thriving BPO industry. Significant cost savings have been made by locating services such as customer support, telephone and online banking, government record storing, and timetable inquiries in India.

Measuring the benefits

In 2007, India's outsourcing industry generated US$33 billion and it is expected to continue growing by broadening the services offered and the types of clients served. Outsourcing is moving up the value chain, adding legal services, hi-tech research, accountancy, medical help, and home or college tuition to the more familiar services. Clients report cost savings of up to 50 percent, but many are drawn to BPO in India for its customer service. In India, BPO typically employs workers who regard it as a high-status position, in contrast to attitudes in the West.

ASK YOURSELF... WOULD OUTSOURCING BENEFIT MY BUSINESS?

- How much of your company's work really needs to be done in-house?
- Are in-house functions like payroll, human resources, bookkeeping, customer response, and technical support core activities that give your business a competitive advantage?
- What impact would transferring these functions to a third-party provider have on your business?
- What impact would up to 50 percent cost savings on these functions have on your business?
- Do your competitors outsource these functions?

CHOOSING THE RIGHT BPO PARTNER

FAST TRACK

OFF TRACK

Meeting a number of potential providers, questioning them closely about their management culture, and focusing on those with a greater understanding of Western business	Being overwhelmed by your first BPO presentation and accepting their offer—they all sound impressive, and most deliver similar service levels
Looking at attrition rates, especially among middle-management—a strong, stable team indicates a good management culture	Believing claims on attrition rates—staff turnover is a major problem for the industry, and most presentations gloss over it
Avoiding risk by seeking long-term relationships with larger, more established BPO providers	Paying attention to short-term cost savings rather than long-term, mutually beneficial relationships

Setting up

Once you've decided to outsource certain non-core functions, the question is: what kind of outsourcing arrangement will best suit your business? There are essentially two options:

• Setting up your own "captive" center, which will work exclusively for your firm. This allows you to retain more control over operations, but it is expensive, and may involve posting members of your management team to India, incurring extra costs for your expat staff, such as accommodation and schooling for their children.

• Contracting a third party—a specialized BPO company—to provide the services for you. This may be an exclusive dedicated provider, or a larger operator who runs many teams, each dedicated to one client.

Whichever model or provider you opt for, data protection will be a key issue—you must protect the privacy of every individual's personal details. Clients will be reassured if you adopt VeriSign or TRUSTe, or the US government's "Safe Harbor" principles—developed to ensure that US companies comply with EU data protection legislation.

Getting started

If you're starting your own business in India, two of the most pressing tasks are registering the company, and finding staff. The government has made great strides in simplifying the bureaucracy involved in registering a new business, but the process is still complex, and takes around one month to complete. Fortunately hiring staff is relatively straightforward—but the challenge lies in retaining them.

Registering the business

You can streamline the many steps involved in registering your business under the guidance of a good local chartered accountant. When choosing your company name, consider a number of alternatives, and check informally at the Register of Companies (ROC) to see if any of these would present issues. The ROC will need to see formal proof that the use of any parent company name has been formally approved by the parent company.

Hiring the right staff

India's unique competitive advantage is a plethora of young people, many of them well-educated and relatively inexpensive to employ. In some sectors, India's labor costs may be as low as an eighth of those in more developed economies. In 2008 you would expect to pay a project leader around US$20,000 in India, compared to approximately US$100,000 in the US; graduates entering BPO call centers were starting on salaries of under US$500 per month, though sought-after technology and management graduates can command far more. Skilled engineers and IT professionals may command up to 75 percent of the salary in the US.

STAFFING IN INDIA

HIRING STAFF

- If you need executive level staff, contact an international recruitment organization with a high profile in India.
- For promising graduates, contact Indian Institutes of Technology and Management directly. They tend to have graduate fairs in January, but you need to build a relationship with the management to get the best students.
- For BPOs, contact the BPO specialists, who provide all forms of BPO solutions, including hiring staff.
- For other types of staff and businesses, you will need to work with a recruitment firm that specializes in your industry. Hire a local consultant to advise which firms are best suited to your needs: retired industrialists are often able and willing to consult.

RETAINING STAFF

- Think of ways to combat boredom and monotony for staff with repetitive tasks.
- Foster team spirit with collective bonuses and team-building weekends.
- Be aware of cultural factors: women, for instance, may feel unable to convince their families of the need to work night shifts.
- Develop honest relationships with staff: never break promises or offer false hope on salaries.

Using contracts and the Indian legal system

India has an independent judiciary and well defined contract law, which has been strengthened by case law. But its judges preside over a failing justice system, beset by corruption and rendered immobile under the weight of huge backlogs.

Avoiding problems

In December 2006, there were more than three million cases pending in the Indian High Courts; and Transparency International's 2005 report found that 77 percent of Indian respondents regarded their judiciary as "corrupt," while 36 percent said they had paid bribes to judges. The World Bank ranked India second-lowest of 178 Asian countries in enforcing contracts in 2004. It is against this background that you must think very carefully about the partners you choose and the type of contracts you sign. When your partner says the contract is not so important to him or her, it is partly because enforcing it in an Indian court would be very difficult. This naturally puts a premium on trust in any agreement, but it also requires additional provisions for enforcement.

CULTURAL ANTENNAE

Trust and contracts

Don't feel that an apparent lack of respect for contracts is a sign of a lack of honesty. Some sectors of the Indian economy have thrived for hundreds of years on extraordinary levels of trust: a good example is the private *hawala* banking trade, where millions of dollars are transferred purely on the trust between two agents thousands of miles from each other. If you wish to succeed in India, resign yourself to the fact that the contract is often seen as a starting point that defines the spirit of the accord; if the context changes, your partner will seek to redefine the terms, and will expect you to be flexible.

Protecting your interests

Support a detailed contract with all relevant documents, such as those discussed in the earlier section "Assessing your partner." These include due diligence reports, self-warranted declarations by your partner, and an alternative dispute resolution mechanism—such as a mediator, Indian or otherwise, who can help resolve any dispute.

In any joint venture, establish clear objectives and make sure your targets are compatible with your partner's. These must be clearly set out in a document known as a "Memorandum of Understanding" or "Heads of Agreement." Attach a Shareholders' Agreement if applicable.

A Memorandum of Understanding, or Heads of Agreement, should include statements on the following: each party's goals; how the venture should develop; the commercial terms—in as much detail as possible, including each party's contribution to the joint venture; management; early costs; the legality of the Memorandum; arbitration; exclusivity.

TIP

TAKE A PROACTIVE APPROACH

Build some contingencies into your contracts to demonstrate generosity of spirit. It will show that you understand the contract is one step on the journey of building a long-term relationship.

Safeguarding your intellectual property

India has, in the past, been identified as a "high-risk area" for theft of intellectual property (IP). But as the Indian R&D economy grows, and software design continues to be a key Indian industry, the government and leading businesses are tightening up on IP protection.

What is protected?

The Indian government has established its own IP protection regime to meet the requirements of the World Trade Organization's Agreement on Trade-Related Aspects of Intellectual Property Rights (TRIPS). Its copyright act protects not just the "authors" of film and the written word, but also the creators of software programs, databases, digital recordings, and satellite broadcasts. The period of protection is 50 years, and the laws are enforced by the Copyright Enforcement Advisory Council. Software copyright is specifically protected, and pirates can be heavily fined and jailed for up to three years. However, India remains a high-risk country for IP theft. You should make full use of the protective laws, but remember that in many cases, the answer lies not so much in a legal remedy as in effective internal security.

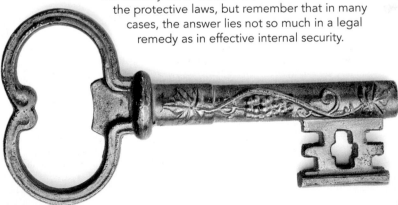

Registering trademarks

India operates a "first to file" policy, so it is important to stake your claim to any mark as soon as possible. Appoint a registered trademark agent to carry out initial searches, then submit your application to the Ministry of Commerce and Industry. If no objection is received within three months of publication, your mark will be registered and the Trademarks Registry will issue a registration certificate. The whole process usually takes two to three years.

TIP

CHECK REPUTATIONS
If you need to protect a product, look for a larger Indian company to work with; ensure that they have a good reputation for honoring licensing agreements, stretching back over several years or longer.

Filing patents

Patenting is a complex procedure in India, taking around four years. The easiest approach is to use a patent agent recommended by the Patent Office. If you file for patent in India within a year of doing so in your own country, your application will be prioritized, and the application backdated to your application date at home. Always work on the assumption that someone will try to steal your creation. Carry out thorough risk assessments and consider hiring IP security specialists to advise you.

IN FOCUS...
FOREIGN TECHNOLOGY TRANSFERS

The Indian government puts a high value on scientific R&D, and its rocket and satellite scientists, engineers, bio-scientists, and IT developers are world class. But there are many areas where India is eager to upgrade its know-how, and the government has drafted rules to help technology transfers. It has agreed a number of technology transfer deals in biotechnology and nuclear energy, aimed at improving its technical standards. If you are interested in selling IP to the government or an Indian organization, payments for technical know-how, designs and drawings, and engineering services are allowed under the "automatic route"—they do not require prior approval from the Indian government.

Resolving disputes

There are four ways to resolve a contractual dispute in India: negotiation, mediation, arbitration, and litigation. However, given the monetary and PR costs of entering the formal dispute process, your best initial tactic may lie in adopting the Indian approach and accepting that the contract is not as important as the relationship.

TIP

RESPECTING THE LAWS

If you outsource to India, ensure that both you and your provider respect the legal systems of both countries: there is no legal system that can be used globally.

Understanding the process

It has become a common feature of foreign investment contracts in India to make provision for arbitration and conciliation overseas. However, it is always worth considering the cost and damage this could cause, and asking yourself whether you would benefit from using a local Indian mediator. As the number of investors in India has multiplied, so has the number of Indian organizations specializing in alternative dispute resolution. Some have specialists with qualifications from Europe and the US, and advisory panels that include retired senior judges. Even if mediation fails to resolve the dispute, it can narrow the gap between the two sides, and minimize the loss in a later arbitration award.

Reaching agreement

India has signed more than 45 bilateral investment treaties with Russia, Japan, Korea, Australia, and most European Union countries. The treaties set out clear provision for disputes to be resolved through negotiation, and if there is no agreement within six months, arbitration. Arbitration may be carried out in India or your home country, or through an international body such as The International Center for the Settlement of Investment Disputes.

Stages in dispute resolution

NEGOTIATION
Most commercial disputes in India are resolved through negotiation. It irks Western investors to renegotiate a contract that they have painstakingly hammered out, but a dispute forces each side to reconsider what the agreement means to them, and to question the value of the overall relationship—is it worth the additional cost of a minor concession?

MEDIATION
When negotiation fails to reach a settlement, an independent conciliator or mediator can be called in to encourage both sides to move closer to the other's position in a non-confrontational atmosphere. The use of mediation has increased rapidly in the last few years, and the process can be beneficial beyond resolving the conflict at hand.

ARBITRATION
If mediation fails, arbitration is the next best solution. The 1996 Arbitration and Conciliation Act enshrines the right of parties to have their disputes settled by arbitration in a foreign jurisdiction—which could be your home country—and for that award to be enforceable in India. These awards are challenged in Indian courts only in exceptional circumstances.

LITIGATION
Resorting to the courts in India is the worst option. It prolongs the dispute, increases the costs, and delays or even ends all hope of reconciliation. If your company is high profile, the public nature of court disputes will mean media coverage, which could intensify ill-will. Even if you achieve a fast resolution from the Court of First Instance, the loser can appeal to three higher courts in succession.

Index

Acknowledgments

Author's acknowledgments

I'd like to thank Subodh Agrawal, Rajesh Dixit, and Raj Chatterjea for their advice and introduction to the global Indian business community. I should acknowledge the influence of Pavan K. Varma's excellent book *Being Indian* for its merciless analysis of Hindu culture and values. And above all, I'd like to thank my wife Pamela, for her research, suggestions, love, and support.

Publisher's acknowledgments

Cobalt id would like to thank Neil Mason, Sarah Tomley, Hilary Bird for indexing, and Charles Wills for co-ordinating Americanization.

Picture credits

The publisher would like to thank the following for their kind permission to reproduce their photographs:

1 Corbis: Jon Hicks; 2–3 iStockphoto.com: Heidi Priesnitz; 4–5 Corbis: Jon Hicks; 8–9 Alamy: Paul Maguire; 11 iStockphoto.com: Marcela Barsse; 12–13 Alamy Images: Jagdish Agarwal/SCPhotos; 15 iStockphoto.com: Edward Grajeda; 17 Alamy: Tim Gainey; 19 Corbis: Strauss/Curtis; 24 iStockphoto.com: Peter Austin; 29 iStockphoto.com: philpell; 31 Alamy: Paul Maguire; 35 iStockphoto.com: Alex Nikada; 37 iStockphoto.com: Rich Seymour; 40 Alamy: Philip Bigg; 41 Alamy: PhotosIndia.com LLC; 45 iStockphoto.com: Bruno Sinnah; 48–49 Alamy: niceartphoto; 50–51 Getty Images: John Brown; 54–55 iStockphoto.com: A-Digit; 63 iStockphoto.com: Bruce Lonngren; 65 iStockphoto.com: Emrah Turudu; 66 iStockphoto.com: Milos Luzanin.

Every effort has been made to trace the copyright holders. The publisher apologizes for any unintentional omission and would be pleased, in such cases, to place an acknowledgment in future editions of this book.